Casper's done some pretty exciting things:

- He's been to the moon with the Apollo 16 Astronauts, who named their command module after him!

- He's working for the United Nations Children's Emergency Fund (UNICEF) to help swell the fund used for needy children around the world!

- He's joined the Boy Scouts of America, to welcome new Cub Scouts into the fold!

- He's been in the movies in many languages!

- He's in eight different comic magazines, read by over 36 million Americans each year—and by many more all over the world in many languages.

- He's on over 400 different items—clothes, food, toys, games!

- He's the star of his very own television show!

- *And now—Casper's in paperback books—just for you!*

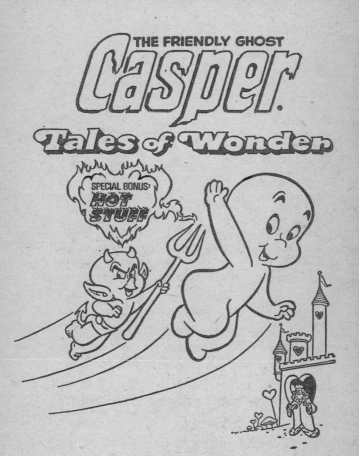

BE *CAREFUL*, CASPER! I SEEM TO REMEMBER THAT A CROCODILE'S *LAUGH* IS A BIGGER *LIE* THAN A CROCODILE'S *TEARS!*

OH... *EVERYONE'S* KNOCKED OUT! SIR GALAHAD, ARE *YOU* ALL RIGHT?

ONE SIDE, GHOST! *YOU'RE* NOT HIS SQUIRE... *I* AM!

AND SOON...

AND SO FAITHFUL PEGASUS BROUGHT ME HERE WITH SIR GALAHAD'S POUCH, YOUR MAJESTY!

HE SOUNDS LIKE A *GRAND* OLD HORSE!

WE SHALL PUT HIM OUT TO *PASTURE* WITH OUR *OTHER FAMOUS* HORSES!

NOW LET US SEE GALAHAD'S NEWS!...*WHAT'S THIS?* APPEALS FOR *HELP* AGAINST THE TERRIBLE *CHAMP 'N' CHOMP!*

MMMM! SMELLS GOOD!

AWP! HEY... GET OUT OF HERE!

ULP! HE WOKE UP!

CASPER and FRIENDS...

HI, FOLKS! I HOPE YOU ENJOYED MY STORIES!

ASK THEM IF THEY LIKED MY STORIES TOO, CASPER!

...AND I HOPE YOU LIKED *HOT STUFF'S* STORIES AND THAT YOU'LL WATCH ALL MY FRIENDS AND ME ON TV!

WHAT'S HAPPENING?

CASPER'S TALKING TO OUR READERS...

...AND THAT YOU'LL READ MORE ABOUT US IN OUR OWN *COMIC BOOKS!*